# CORETTA SCOTT KING

## CIVIL RIGHTS ACTIVIST

"There is no problem that we can't solve
if we can corral our resources behind it.
That means people, that means money,
that means the good will and cooperation
of a large segment of people."
— Coretta Scott King

BY CYNTHIA KLINGEL

**The Child's World®**
childsworld.com

Published by The Child's World®
1980 Lookout Drive • Mankato, MN 56003-1705
800-599-READ • www.childsworld.com

**CONTENT CONSULTANT**
Kira Duke, former Education Coordinator,
National Civil Rights Museum

**PHOTOS**
Cover and page 4: AP Photo/Harvey Georges
Interior: akg-images/Arthur Rothstein/Newscom: 15; AP Photo: 11, 20; AP
Photo/384289Globe Photos/MediaPunch/IPX: 23; AP Photo/Atlanta Journal-
Constitution, File: 17, 29 (left); AP Photo/Charles Tasnadi: 26; AP Photo/Gene Herrick:
16, 19, 28 (right); AP Photo/Harry Cabluck: 21, 31; AP Photo/Jim Bourdier: 24; AP
Photo/Ric Feld, File: 27, 29 (right); Arnie Sachs/CNP/Newscom: 25; Arthur Rothstein/
Library of Congress, Prints and Photographs Division: 5; C5 Media/Shutterstock.com:
14; Dorothea Lange/Library of Congress, Prints and Photographs Division: 6; Everett
Collection/Newscom: 18; Everett Collection/Shutterstock.com: 7; Herman Hiller/
Library of Congress, Prints and Photographs Division: 13; Library of Congress, Prints
and Photographs Division: 10, 12, 28 (left); Marion Post Wolcott/Library of Congress,
Prints and Photographs Division: 8, 9; Sam Melhorn/ZUMA Press/Newscom: 22

**LIBRARY OF CONGRESS CATALOGING-IN-PUBLICATION DATA**
ISBN 9781503854444 (Reinforced Library Binding)
ISBN 9781503854901 (Portable Document Format)
ISBN9781503855281 (Online Multi-user eBook)
LCCN: 2021930430

Printed in the United States of America

Cover and page 4 caption:
Coretta Scott King at a
news conference in 1976.

# CONTENTS

## Chapter One

# A BETTER LIFE

As a young girl, Coretta Scott lived with her family in a tiny home with only two rooms—a kitchen and a bedroom. It was a small place for five people. The floors were bare wood, and the paper peeled off the walls. The family carried water from a well in the backyard. It wasn't very different from how other Black families lived in Alabama at the time. But Coretta's parents, Obadiah (Obie) Scott and Bernice McMurry Scott, wanted more for their family.

Coretta was born on April 27, 1927, two years before the **Great Depression** began. During the Depression, thousands of Americans lost their jobs, and many people barely had enough to eat. The Scotts didn't have much money, but they did have a small farm where they could raise animals and grow vegetables. The entire family helped on the farm to make sure they always had food on the table.

A young girl looks out of her window in Alabama in 1937.

The Great Depression was a time of economic hardship partly caused by the **stock market crash** of 1929. Many people lost large amounts of money, and many banks and businesses failed.

Coretta's older sister was Edythe. They had a younger brother, Obie, who was named after their father. All three of the Scott children woke up at dawn to feed the chickens and hogs. They milked the cows before it was time to go to school. In the summer, they helped their mother tend a large vegetable garden. The children also earned money by chopping wood and picking cotton for neighbors.

Coretta's father worked the hardest of all. In addition to running the family farm, he worked long hours at a lumber mill. He even opened a small barbershop in their home. After saving enough money to buy a truck, Obie Scott began hauling lumber for the mill operator at night and on weekends.

No matter how hard the Scotts worked, things were not easy for them—or for other Black families who lived in the South during the 1930s. Obie Scott was the only Black man in the county who owned a truck. White truck owners were afraid he would take business away from them, and they often threatened him.

People shopping on a busy North Carolina street in 1939.

After much effort, Obie Scott finally saved enough money to buy his own lumber mill. When a white man tried to buy it from him, Obie refused. A few days later, the mill was burned to the ground. Obie Scott realized that he had put himself in danger by trying to build a better life for his family.

Members of the Ku Klux Klan attend a nighttime ceremony in 1921.

Even though the Scott family faced hatred from the white people in their town, Obie refused to stop working hard. Because of Obie's dedication, his family was able to move into a much bigger home when Coretta was ten years old. The house had six rooms, which made it feel like a palace to the Scott family. There was a living room with fine new furniture, and Coretta and Edythe shared a bedroom.

Only five years later, it was all gone. On Thanksgiving Day in 1942, the family's beautiful home burned down. The Scotts felt certain that the white men who had threatened Obie for some time were responsible. But they believed it would do no good to ask the sheriff to investigate. It seemed as though no one cared what happened to Black people in the South.

The Ku Klux Klan is a secretive group that started in the South after the Civil War. Its members believe in white supremacy and gaining power through acts of terror. They have been accused of setting fire to properties, lynching, and threatening Black people and other minorities.

The house fire was the most difficult act of **prejudice** that the Scott family endured, but it certainly wasn't the first.

## Chapter Two

# STRUGGLING FOR AN EDUCATION

When Coretta was growing up in the South, white and Black people were **segregated** from each other. Black children couldn't go to school with white children or even drink from the same water fountains. At the movies, Coretta and her friends had to sit in the hot, crowded balcony. White children could sit in comfortable seats on the main floor.

Edythe, Coretta, and young Obie attended the Crossroads School in Heiberger, Alabama. It was a school for Black children in the area. Every day, rain or shine, they walked about three miles (5 km) to school. As they walked, the school bus rumbled past, carrying white children to their own, separate school.

Students study in a one-room schoolhouse in Alabama in 1939.

A Black man enters a theater through the "colored" door in Mississippi in the 1930s.

Coretta knew the white children had a nice brick school with different rooms for each grade and a library filled with books. At the Crossroads School, more than 100 children were crowded into a single, shabby room. Two teachers struggled to teach six grades, and there were never enough books for all of the students.

With these problems, it wasn't easy for the children at Coretta's school to complete all six grades. It was almost impossible for them to continue on to high school. The closest high school for Black students was 20 miles (32 km) from the Scotts' home. There were no school buses for Black students, although white students were bused to Marion High School, which was only ten miles (16 km) away.

Coretta's mother, Bernice, had only a fourth grade education. She was determined to send her children to high school. Bernice arranged for Coretta and Edythe to stay with a family in Marion, where they could attend Lincoln School, a private high school for Black students.

Antioch College in 1933.

At first, the Scott girls were the only Black children from their community fortunate enough to attend high school. Most families couldn't afford to pay for their children's housing and living costs in faraway Marion. Then, when Coretta was a junior in high school, her father converted one of his trucks into a makeshift bus. Although it meant a 40-mile (64-km) trip each day, Bernice drove all the Black children from their area to and from school. Not only could more children attend Lincoln School, but Coretta could also return home to live with her family.

Antioch College was founded in 1852. Horace Mann, its first president, declared, "Be ashamed to die until you win some victory for humanity." The phrase is now the college **motto.**

Lincoln School opened a whole new world to Coretta. It was as good as the white high schools in the area. The teachers, some of whom were white, believed Black children deserved an education equal to that of white children. Some people in Marion threatened the white teachers and called them names for choosing to teach and work with Black people.

Coretta earned top grades in all her subjects, but she enjoyed music most of all. Her teachers complimented her beautiful voice. She took voice lessons, sang in the choir, and learned to play the trumpet and the piano. During her senior year in 1945, Coretta

Coretta Scott (number 355) at Antioch College in 1945

learned that she had won a **scholarship** to Antioch College in Yellow Springs, Ohio. Edythe had received a scholarship and was already a student at Antioch. Coretta was happy to join her. Coretta was also ready to leave the South. She knew that Black people struggled less against **racism** and prejudice in the northern states.

Coretta's years at Antioch went quickly as she continued to study music. She was one of only six Black students but made friends with all her classmates. She had planned to become a teacher, but during her last year at Antioch, her professors urged her to continue studying music. They thought she was talented enough to become a concert singer. Before graduating, Coretta applied to study at the New England Conservatory of Music in Boston.

## Chapter Three

# MEETING MARTIN LUTHER KING JR.

In 1951, Coretta won a small scholarship to attend the New England Conservatory of Music, but she still needed to earn money to help pay for school. She kept a busy schedule studying, attending classes, and working at small jobs. In 1952, she received financial aid from the state of Alabama. Coretta was able to stop working so much and devote more time to her studies. The money was given only to Black college students who studied at schools outside the state. Those who chose to study at Alabama colleges were not eligible for the state's financial aid. The system seemed to encourage Black students to leave the state.

Coretta Scott King in 1964

In Boston, Coretta's studies kept her busy. She didn't have many opportunities to meet people, and sometimes she was lonely. In 1952, Coretta's friend Mary Powell told her about a young man named Martin Luther King Jr. from Atlanta, Georgia. He was a minister studying at Boston University. King had asked Powell if she knew any kind, attractive young women. When Powell told him about Coretta, King wanted to meet her.

Coretta agreed to have lunch with King. They liked each other, and soon they were spending as much time together as their studies would allow. King often mentioned marriage, but Coretta was not interested at first. She wanted to pursue a career as an opera singer, and it was clear that King wanted a wife who would put their marriage and family first.

The more King talked about his goals in life, the more Coretta realized they were the same as hers. Like Coretta, he wanted to help Black people get a quality education and decent jobs. He wanted to help them achieve **civil rights**. Coretta agreed to marry King, even though it meant giving up the possibility of a singing career. In 1953, less than a year after they met, Coretta and King were married in a ceremony at her family's home. After the wedding, the couple returned to Boston to complete their studies. King received his PhD from Boston University.

> Martin Luther King Jr. graduated from Morehouse College in Atlanta, Georgia, in 1948. He then received a divinity degree from Crozer Theological Seminary before attending Boston University.

The Kings in 1964.

Dexter Avenue Baptist Church in Montgomery, Alabama

Once he finished school, Dr. King had many job offers. Several of them were in the North. After living in Boston, the newlywed couple knew it would be difficult to return to the segregated South, but they agreed it was their duty to return. Their efforts could make the most difference in the South. In 1954, Dr. King accepted a position as a pastor at the Dexter Avenue Baptist Church in Montgomery, Alabama. The couple's first child, Yolanda, was born the next year, in 1955.

## Chapter Four

# BACK IN THE SOUTH

Coretta had nearly forgotten what life was like for Black people in the South. In Alabama, she and Dr. King had to use elevators, drinking fountains, and restrooms marked "colored," which was the term used at the time to describe Black people. They had to eat in separate restaurants. They couldn't enter public buildings through the same door as white people.

Black people had to use a separate balcony at this Alabama movie theater in 1940.

Rosa Parks was dedicated to the fight for racial equality. She and her husband were members of the National Association for the Advancement of Colored People (NAACP). She was elected secretary of the Montgomery chapter of the organization.

The Montgomery Bus Company had its own set of unfair rules. The seats in the front of the buses were for whites only. Black people had to sit in the back of the bus. If all the front seats in the bus were taken, Black riders had to give up their seats to whites. Black people even had to pay their fares at the front of the bus, get off, and then board again through the rear door. Sometimes a driver would pull away without the Black passenger after he or she had already paid the fare.

On December 1, 1955, a Black woman named Rosa Parks refused to give up her bus seat to a white man. The police arrested Parks and took her to jail. The Black citizens of Montgomery decided that segregated buses had operated long enough. Many wondered what would happen if Black people stopped riding city buses in protest. The Women's Political Council suggested the idea of a bus **boycott**. A message was passed among the city's 50,000 Black people telling them not to ride city buses to work, town, school, or anywhere else on Monday, December 5, 1955.

Rosa Parks arrives at court on March 19, 1956.

On the day of the boycott, Dr. King and Coretta were up at 5:30 in the morning. The first bus was due to drive past their house in 30 minutes. As its headlights pierced the darkness, Coretta stood at the window, straining to see inside the bus. There was not a single person on the usually crowded bus. Almost no one rode the bus that day. Some people went to work in cars, others on foot. Some took taxis or rode bicycles, and some even arrived at their destinations in horse-drawn buggies.

Coretta and Dr. King with their four children: Dexter (left), Yolanda (standing), Bernice, and Martin Luther King III.

That afternoon, many of the community's Black leaders met to create a list of their demands. They did not ask that Black people be permitted to sit anywhere they wanted on Montgomery buses. Instead, they asked only that bus drivers treat them politely and that Black riders not be forced to give up their seats to whites. They also asked that Black drivers drive the buses in Black neighborhoods. The group resolved to encourage the community to boycott the Montgomery Bus Company until these goals were reached.

The group also asked Dr. King to be their president. He was a very powerful speaker, and many people respected him. This was the beginning of Dr. King's important work in the **civil rights movement**.

The Montgomery Improvement Association organized a meeting that evening, and 5,000 Black people attended. They agreed to continue the boycott until the demands were met. Black citizens of Montgomery knew they were in for a long struggle.

Marting Luther King Jr. speaks after being elected leader of the Montgomery Improvement Association in 1956.

Coretta kisses her husband on the cheek after they leave the courtroom in Montgomery, Alabama, in 1956.

The bus boycott lasted for more than one year. This was a difficult time for Black Americans in Montgomery. Many people were angry about the boycott, and one day someone threw a bomb at the Kings' house. Although no one was hurt, the experience scared the family. Dr. King and Coretta still refused to back down.

In 1956, a U.S. **Supreme Court** order put a stop to the unfair rules of the Montgomery Bus Company. By that time, requests for Dr. King to help organize other nonviolent protests were pouring in from across the nation. The boycott had shown what people could do if they united to fight for their rights without resorting to violence.

## Chapter Five

# A DANGEROUS PATH

As the civil rights movement grew, Dr. King resigned from his position at the church. The family moved to Atlanta, Georgia, so Dr. King could lead the Southern Christian Leadership Conference (SCLC). This organization was created to combat segregation and other injustices. The SCLC used nonviolent methods and tried to help the civil rights movement gain support.

Dr. King had been offered many jobs with high salaries, but he had turned them down. He took no money from the SCLC. The King family lived on a small income from Ebenezer Baptist Church, where King's father was the pastor and he was co-pastor.

Coretta speaking at a rally for peace in Washington, DC.

People frequently asked Dr. King to speak at events around the country and to help organize nonviolent protests. As Dr. King's responsibilities grew, so did the demands on Coretta. The Kings now had four small children: Yolanda, Martin Luther III, Dexter, and Bernice. Not only was Coretta busy at home, but she also traveled with her husband.

In addition, Coretta had found a way to use her musical talent. She gave a performance at New York City's Town Hall using poetry, dramatic readings, protest songs, and **spirituals** to tell the story of the civil rights movement. The audience found the combination of words and songs effective and inspiring. Coretta soon received requests from across the nation for more "Freedom Concerts."

Coretta shared her husband's belief that the problems Black people experienced could be solved through nonviolence. She also believed the civil rights movement was part of a larger goal: world peace. In 1962, she was named a **delegate** to the Women's Strike for Peace in Geneva, Switzerland.

> In the 1960s, the United States and Russia were testing nuclear weapons. Coretta had a part in the Women's Strike for Peace, which rallied against the testing of these weapons. Many women were concerned about the health risks nuclear weapons would pose for children.

Coretta studies the words and melody to a protest song in 1965.

Even though Coretta was traveling a great deal, the needs of her family always came first. More and more, Dr. King's work took him away from home. Coretta fully understood the dangers her husband faced each day. Many southerners strongly opposed the idea that Black Americans deserved civil rights, and Dr. King's efforts angered them. Sometimes they attacked him. Other times the police arrested him during protests. Coretta feared for her husband's safety, but she truly believed he was doing the right thing.

On April 4, 1968, Martin Luther King Jr. was **assassinated** in Memphis, Tennessee. Dr. King had gone to Memphis to support a strike by Black sanitation workers. He was shot while on the balcony outside his hotel room. He was 39 years old.

Coretta and three of her children led a memorial march through downtown Memphis after Martin Luther King's funeral on April 8, 1968.

Coretta spoke after her husband's funeral in 1968.

Coretta had suffered a lot by this time, but she remained strong. The next day, she made a statement to the press. Coretta told the people that both she and her husband had known his life might be cut short. They both felt it was not how long one lived that was important, but how well one lived.

Coretta urged those who had admired her husband to help carry on his work. The day before his funeral, she took Dr. King's place in a civil rights march he was to have led in Memphis. Thousands of people joined her from across the country. Thousands more stood along the route in silent tribute to the memory of a courageous leader and the bravery of his widow.

The day before Dr. King was assassinated, there had been a bomb threat on his flight to Memphis. He gave a speech later that night and stated, "And so I'm happy, tonight. I'm not worried about anything. I'm not fearing any man. Mine eyes have seen the glory of the coming of the Lord!"

## Chapter Six

# IN DR. KING'S MEMORY

After Dr. Martin Luther King Jr.'s death, Coretta committed herself even more firmly to the goals she had shared with her husband. She knew that when she had married Dr. King, she had united herself to the causes he felt so strongly about. Those causes included equality for Black people. She realized how important it was that she continue to do not only her own work but her husband's as well. She went in his place to events that he had planned to attend. At a peace rally in New York, she spoke from his notes. Just months after his death, Coretta called upon American women to unite to fight racism, poverty, and war.

Coretta sings at a memorial service for Martin Luther King, Jr. on June 4, 1968.

Coretta was not afraid to speak to crowds and media.

That same year, she founded the Martin Luther King Jr., Center for Nonviolent Social Change (known as the King Center) as a memorial to her husband. Located in Atlanta, Georgia, the King Center has continued to grow. More than 650,000 people visit it every year. Visitors learn about King's ideas and goals. Coretta was the president of the organization until her son Dexter took over the position in 1995. She continued to dedicate much of her time to the King Center, which sponsors programs and events in the name of world peace, human rights, and freedom.

The first Coretta Scott King Book Award was presented in 1970 to a book named *Martin Luther King, Jr.: Man of Peace* by Lillie Patterson.

Coretta joined others in Washington DC to protest the practice of apartheid in South Africa.

Over the years, Coretta served on many political committees. Various organizations recognized that her and her husband's vision for nonviolent social change greatly contributed to the civil rights movement. President Jimmy Carter appointed her to several positions, including a one-year assignment to the United Nations in 1977. The Coretta Scott King Book Award, which honors her courage and determination, is awarded yearly to Black authors and illustrators of outstanding and inspirational books. These books highlight an aspect of the experiences of Black Americans.

In 1985, Coretta and two of her children, Bernice and Martin III, were arrested outside the South African Embassy in Washington, DC. Just as Dr. King had led protests against the mistreatment of Black Americans, the King family was protesting racism that was happening outside of the United States. Coretta, Bernice, and Martin III protested **apartheid**, the policy of strict segregation imposed on Black South Africans. Coretta showed that she was focused on achieving equality around the world.

For years, Coretta worked to make Dr. King's birthday a national holiday. In 1986, Congress approved the plan. Martin Luther King Jr. Day is held on the third Monday of January. It is the first American holiday dedicated to a Black American. After the holiday was established, Coretta continued to attend fundraisers and events focused on racial equality.

In August of 2005, Coretta suffered a mild heart attack. She was also battling cancer. She was sent to a health care clinic in Mexico for treatment. Coretta Scott King died on January 30, 2006.

During her lifetime, Coretta Scott King received more than 60 **honorary doctorates** from colleges and universities. She is recognized as one of America's most influential leaders. Her fight to bring a nonviolent end to prejudice in the United States will long be remembered.

After Martin Luther King Jr. Day was established, Coretta testified before the U.S. Senate. She told members of a special committee that the national holiday should be a day in which Americans dedicate their time to public service, not to recreation.

Coretta speaks at Atlanta's Ebenezer Baptist Church in 2005 to honor Martin Luther King Jr. Day.

It would be easy for a woman like Coretta Scott King
to be defined by her husband and his work.
But she fought for civil rights and equality long after his death.
How would you put her contributions into your own words?

As a child, both Coretta's family home and her father's mill
were destroyed when white men set them on fire.
But no one was ever punished for these crimes.
Why do you think this is?

## TIME LINE

### 1920-1939

**1927**
Coretta Scott is born in
Heiberger, Alabama,
on April 27.

**1929**
The Great Depression begins.

**1937**
The Scotts move into a new
and larger home.

### 1940-1959

**1942**
The Scotts' home burns down.

**1945**
Coretta enrolls at Antioch
College.

**1951**
Coretta leaves Antioch
College for Boston,
Massachusetts, where she
attends the New England
Conservatory of Music.

**1952**
Coretta meets Martin Luther
King Jr.

**1953**
Coretta and King marry
in Marion, Alabama.

**1954**
Dr. King accepts a job as
the minister of the Dexter
Avenue Baptist Church in
Montgomery, Alabama.

**1955**
Rosa Parks is arrested for
refusing to give up her seat to a
white man. The Montgomery
Bus Boycott begins.

**1956**
The U.S. Supreme Court
rules that segregated buses
are unconstitutional.

**Coretta attended a great high school,
but not all Black students were so lucky.**
What happens when some kids are not allowed to get a good education?

**Mrs. King believed that nonviolent methods
could help in the fight for civil rights.**
What are some examples of nonviolent action?

## 1960-1979

**1962**
Coretta attends the Women's Strike for Peace in Geneva, Switzerland.

**1968**
Dr. King is assassinated.

**1970**
The first Coretta Scott King Book Award is presented.

## 1980-1999

**1981**
The Martin Luther King, Jr., Center for Nonviolent Social Change opens in Atlanta, Georgia. Coretta is president of the center.

**1985**
Coretta and her children Bernice and Martin III are arrested during a protest against apartheid.

**1986**
Dr. King's birthday becomes a national holiday.

## 2000

**2006**
Coretta Scott King dies on January 30.

**apartheid (uh-PART-hate)**
Apartheid is the former policy of the South African government of separating Black and white people. Coretta was arrested for protesting apartheid.

**assassinated (uh-SASS-uh-nay-ted)**
When an important or well-known person is assassinated, he or she is murdered. Coretta's husband, Dr. Martin Luther King Jr., was assassinated in 1968.

**boycott (BOY-kot)**
To boycott means not using a certain product or service as a form of protest. Coretta and Dr. King participated in a bus boycott.

**civil rights (SIV-il RITES)**
Civil rights are personal freedoms that belong to all U.S. citizens. Coretta was a pioneer for civil rights.

**civil rights movement (SIV-il RITES MOOV-munt)**
The civil rights movement is the name given to the struggle for equal rights for Black people in the United States during the 1950s and 1960s. Coretta and her family participated in the civil rights movement.

**delegate (DEL-uh-gut)**
A delegate is a person who is named as a representative to an important event. Coretta served as a delegate to the Women's Strike for Peace.

**Great Depression (GRAYT di-PRESH-un)**
The Great Depression was a period of economic turmoil from 1929 through the early 1940s. Coretta was born two years before the Great Depression began.

**honorary doctorates (ON-uh-rayr-ee DOK-tur-ets)**
Honorary doctorates are degrees given as an award to a person who has notable accomplishments. Coretta received more than 60 honorary doctorates.

**lynching (LINCH-ing)**
Lynching is a means of putting a person to death, often by hanging, without legal cause. The Ku Klux Klan has been accused of lynching Black people in the South.

**motto (MAH-toh)**
A motto is a sentence or phrase that states what a person or group believes in. Horace Mann created the motto for Antioch College, where Coretta attended school.

**prejudice (PREJ-uh-diss)**
Prejudice is a negative feeling or opinion about someone without just cause. The Scott family faced prejudice in Alabama when Coretta was growing up.

**racism (RAY-sih-zum)**
Racism is the belief that one race is superior to another. The Scott family experienced racism when whites set fire to their home.

**scholarship (SKAHL-ur-ship)**
A scholarship is an award of money given to a successful student to be used toward his or her education. Coretta received a scholarship to attend Antioch College.

**segregated (SEG-ruh-gay-ted)**
To be segregated is to keep race, class, or ethnic groups apart. When Coretta was growing up, life was segregated in the South.

**spirituals (SPEER-uh-choo-ulz)**
Religious songs written by enslaved Black people in the southern United States are called spirituals. Coretta had a beautiful singing voice and sang many spirituals.

**stock market (STOK MAR-kit)**
The stock market is where shares of companies are bought and sold. The stock market crash of 1929 partly caused the Great Depression.

**Supreme Court (suh-PREEM KORT)**
The Supreme Court is the most powerful court in the United States. A Supreme Court order stopped segregation on Montgomery buses.

**white supremacy (WITE suh-PREM-uh-see)**
People who believe in white supremacy believe that the white race is better than other races. The Ku Klux Klan believes in white supremacy.

## BOOKS

Calkhoven, Laurie. *DK Life Stories: Martin Luther King Jr.*
New York, NY: DK Publishing, 2019.

Herman, Gail. *Who Was Coretta Scott King?*
New York. NY: Penguin Group USA 2017.

Hooks, Gwendolyn. *If You Were a Kid During the Civil Rights Movement*. New York, NY: Children's Press, 2017.

Krull, Kathleen. *Women Who Broke the Rules: Coretta Scott King.*
New York, NY: Bloomsbury, 2015.

Shange, Ntozake. *Coretta Scott*. Norwalk, CT: Scholastic, 2013.

Venable, Rose. *The Civil Rights Movement*. Mankato, MN: The Child's World, 2021.

## WEBSITES

Visit our website for links about Coretta Scott King:

### childsworld.com/links

*Note to Parents, Teachers, and Librarians: We routinely verify our Web links to make sure they are safe, active sites—so encourage your readers to check them out!*